Run Away Home

A journey through life...so far

Toni Lynn Britton

D1089566

Wider Perspectives Publishing ¤ 2022 ¤ Hampton Roads, Va.

© April 2022, Toni Lynn Britton, Norfolk, VA.
Wider Perspectives Publishing, Hampton Roads
ISBN 978-1-952773-54-9

Please follow Toni B. at
https://tonib19695.wixsite.com/rawdatablogger
or Instagram as @rawdatablogger

Run Away Home

A journey through life...so far

Toni Lynn Britton

Dedicated To...

My parents – love and gratitude, always.
You always gave the very best you had and
none of that is lost on me.

My family – you know who you are. I remain
eternally grateful for each of you.

My readers – Namaste. We are connected through
this human condition, and you are not alone.

Contents

Grief

Run Away Home

Preface

In 2009, I began to write a book. It was going to be an autobiography with the title "Run Away Home" and an underlying theme of finding oneself. I had so many elements to include from my marriage, our walk with cancer, my emergence as a widow, and finding myself. Interestingly, I could not make that book happen. It wasn't until now, 2021, that I finally realized I was writing the wrong book.

I had been writing about "our" life. But to really find my theme, I had to find **my** voice. I could not speak for him. I had to speak for me, from my vantage point. While writing has always been an important part of my life. I did not find the strength of my voice until very recently. Each section of this book begins with a poem from my youth and is followed by selections of my path toward healing.

This life is a journey filled with twists and turns and massive pendulum swings. It isn't always pretty, and it isn't always easy, but it is a gift. We can choose to open it and enjoy it, leave it in the box, or exchange it for something else. At one time or another, I'm sure I have done all three...

~Toni B.

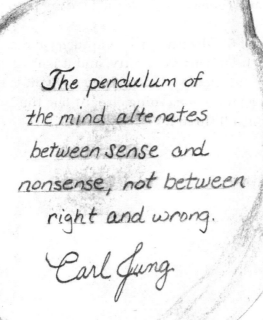

The pendulum of
the mind alternates
between sense and
nonsense, not between
right and wrong.

Carl Jung

Act 1
Family

I have always loved my family the best way I knew how
at each point in the journey.

As with all humans, family is our foundation and our blessing...as
well as our curse. The following is a collection of writings where I
have come to terms with the things my family has taught me. Or,
perhaps more precisely, I have come to terms with my choices
with the information I gathered from my family.

Love is something people give in the way they understand it. I
have always been loved by my family from the places they were
able to love.

I am eternally grateful for everything.

Toni B.

My Cat

(Sept. 2, 1987 – age 18)

They won't let me grow up
        Or think for myself
        But, still, they say they love me

I cannot make decisions
        If they differ even a little
        But, still, they say they care

I am given rights only in words
        My actions must be as theirs
        But they say I am my own person

I can do what I want to
        The choices are mine to make
        But they must ultimately be approved

Well, I've decided to choose
        To make my own rights
        Even if they don't agree

And when all is said and done
        They will both cry
        But I think I'll miss my cat.

First Word

I don't think I can prove it
But it must somehow be true
My first word ever spoken
Wasn't mama nor dada, it had to be "no"
For everything I wanted to be
The answer was the same
"Can I..." – no
"I'd like to..." – no
"I've always wanted to..." – no
No
No
I wasn't asking for the world
Just for some room to fly
It became a constant message
Ever looping in my mind
Everything I wanted to be
Was not considered good for me
I should know better
Learn a trade
Be responsible
Make an honest living
Their words became my own
Everything I'd start to try
Eventually got cast aside
I didn't even realize
I was telling myself, "No"
Gave up on myself
So very easily

Toni B.

Steady, stable, practical
Became a way of life for me
But none of it fulfilled the call
That still beckons from my soul
Steady, stable, practical
Isn't meant to be my role
My wings are always straining
Because my feet are in concrete
I need to break away the weight
And finally, be free
Though my first word was probably
A very fervent NO
Today I am replacing that
With, "YES! Come on, let's go!"

I am My Father's Daughter

Friendliness has been in my blood since birth.

My dad never met a stranger. He would talk to anyone. Waitresses, cashiers, even passersby. He would smile and joke and entertain. I loved that about him – his people-ease was amazing. It taught me to love people and it showed me that sometimes others are helped in some small way by a kind word or smile, a nod or handshake or wink. He had an amazing way about him, and he made other people's day a little brighter if only for a few moments.

My mother, on the other hand, grew tired and annoyed by him. I would see her standing back and giving him a look and biting her tongue. I didn't understand her annoyance. I didn't understand that she saw something different and intrusive about the way he approached strangers and she saw something different in their responses. I only saw my daddy loving the entire world. And I saw how my dad looked at my mom like she was the queen of the world. He went to work and came home to her.

Sometimes, he would stop the car alongside the road and get out leaving the car running and the three of us sitting there. He'd run around the side of the road with a big smile and pick a bunch of tiger lilies growing wild only to run back to the car and hand them to my mom with a big grin then kiss her on the cheek. Then he'd put the car in drive, and we would continue on to wherever we were going. I am my father's daughter.

My mom, though, for as long as I can recall and up through his cancer complained about him. One day, as an adult, I asked my

7

Toni B.

mom why she ever married him in the first place. I mean, she was so often annoyed by him for just being him. And her answer confused me even more. She loved him and married him because of his personality – that fun-loving, friendly, outgoing nature that he passed on to me is exactly what drew her to him in 1964. That talkative – no secrets – put-it-out-there people-ease of my father was infectious. It is what she fell in love with and admired. And yet, after 30, 40, 50 years, it was what she disliked the most. I did not understand that, but I also get it. Opposites attract, after all. It's what makes for the dynamic energy exchange that allows for the delicate dance between love and hate. Igniting the soul and electrifying the space.

I am my father's daughter. I enjoy the stage of life – but I never forget where home is.

I am my father's daughter

I am my mother's sun

I am by brother's shadow

I am my future begun

ToniB @rawdatablogger

Toni B.

When My Mother Smiles

When I think about my mother
Many things come to mind
But the moment I go back to most
Was a moment in the kitchen
She was a master of the room
Scratch cook who taught me
Everything she could
Everything I would take in
This particular moment
She stood by the stove
Stirring something wonderful
Though what it was I can't recall
I stood alongside her
Chatter, chatter, chatter
I was always performing
I don't know what I was talking about
It doesn't really matter
But suddenly she smiled and laughed
A small laugh while she stirred
It was a magic moment
I lived for moments like this
I asked her what was so funny
And she just shook her head
"You just have a knack," she said
For what, I didn't know
"A knack for making people smile."
Is what she said to me
She never looked up from that pot
She just kept stirring away
I didn't keep on speaking

My work here was done
I made my biggest fan in life
Smile and laugh, small victory, I won
She was quite the worker
Diligent in everything
Our house was clean,
Our meals were good
Our family provided for
But it was serious work to her
The times when I could make her smile
Were trophies in my case
It proved to me that happiness
Still existed in her gait
That's all I ever wanted for her
To smile and enjoy
For life seemed to be a heavy weight
She picked up every morn'
Sometimes I wish she'd shown me more
Of the silly she must possess
I'd like to have seen her friendships
And the pursuit of her dreams
Though I'm grateful for the constant care
She truly was amazing
I hope that she can also be
The carefree girl her heart sings
For she is such a beauty
With her lighthearted smile
She doesn't show it often
It's a sight to behold
For when my mother really smiles
It shines like purest gold

Dreams

I had some dreams
They were clouds in my coffee
Clouds in my coffee, and
I had to let them go
Not practical
Convinced myself that some things
Are best just kept as dreams
The cost would be too great
Sour grapes
Self-deflate
At the tender age of four
You could find me performing
To the audience in my mind
I'd put the records on
And sing for hours on end
Mommy did you catch the show?
She was always busy you know
But the audience in my mind
Cheered me on kept in time
Chances are you believe the stars
That fill the skies are in my eyes.
Ah, but the stars were out of my reach
Sparkling so high in the sky
Daddy didn't help me fly
Kept my feet firmly on the ground
My wings with practicality were bound
So maybe dreams are only that
Escapes from the life your parents craft
But if that's true then why is this dream
Seeded so deeply inside of me

Maybe mom and dad were wrong
Because they didn't understand my song
For the only times I feel alive
Are when I write and sing through life
Give me a stage and an audience of even one
And I will stand and sing my song
Even though I'll soon be fifty-three
Perhaps it's not too late for me
To Sing, Sing a song
Make it simple
To last your whole life long
Don't worry if it's not good enough
For anyone else to hear
Just sing

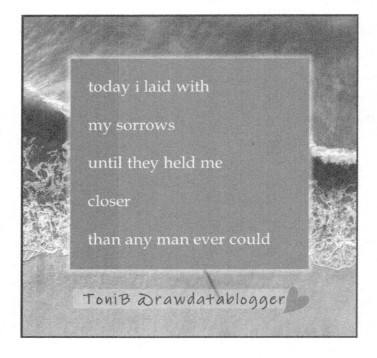

today i laid with

my sorrows

until they held me

closer

than any man ever could

ToniB @rawdatablogger

The F Word

You think you know the F word?
Fuck!
Fuck this!
Fuck that!
Fuck everything!
Fuck...me

Nah. That's not the F word
At least it's not to me
Family is the original F word
I swear

My family taught me
Some jacked up shit
Like, those that love you the most
Will hurt you
Mentally
Physically
Verbally
Sexually

Yeah, I can take a punch
You said you made me tough
But you never considered
That's not the kind of tough I want to be
Can't put "can take a punch" on no résumé

But man, my résumé, in life
Used that as a headline

Toni B.

You said you made me tough?
Ha!
Laughable
You made me think
That was love

Family is the original F word
I swear

"Sex has always been
An open topic
In our family"
Isn't that what you told me?
When I was only eight?
Funny
I don't recall a conversation
This shit is pornography
Given freely to me
A child with curiosity
You didn't teach me about sex
You taught me about shame
You taught me about
What I was supposed to look like
But didn't
You taught me debauchery

Family is the original F word
I swear

"Actually, I always wanted two boys"
Isn't that what you told me
When I was only four?

It didn't matter what you said after that
I was four
You told me
I wasn't what you wanted

I learned **I wasn't enough**
I **learned** I wasn't enough
I learned I wasn't enough

Family is the original F word
I swear

"We can only be in contact for
'Necessary business'
Otherwise, you are dead to us"
Isn't that what you said to me
When I was 18
And got my first tiny wings?

Funny
You could never tell me
What business was necessary
Evidently only **your** business.
Until someone asked you
Twelve years later
"Who's to say what is necessary
Business with your daughter?"
Wait!
What!?
Someone had to ask you that
For you to pick up the damn phone?!

Family is the original F word
I swear

A child believes without proof
Parents and siblings will protect them
But parents and siblings expose them
To their own devils and demons

Generational curses
Passed down as right,
Accepted as what is
That's life
Well, I call bullshit!

Through all of this
And so much more
I was constantly shown
So many ridiculous ideas
About right and wrong
About good and evil
About worth
I learned **I wasn't enough**
I **learned** I wasn't enough
I learned I wasn't enough

Family is the original F word
I swear

Before words like
Fun, fantastic, or foundation
There was family

And I am part of this family
Just as much as
Any other member
In all of the stories
No matter how ugly
I was a key member

In each situation
I was present

In each teachable moment
I had a choice
In each chosen silence
I gave away my voice

Family is the original F word
I swear
But my favorite F word is
FORGIVENESS
For that brings freedom
And when we become free
Then we can truly LOVE

And so, I must forgive
MYSELF
For giving away those things
No one was trying to steal
For quieting my truth
And dimming my light
For knowing better
And not doing better

Toni B.

Because the truth is
There is no fault
Only choices

Yes, family is the original F word
And I swear
I shall be
Continually
Grateful
For mine.

Untitled Tragedy

I am the baby of the family
Of the baby of the family
Carrying the scars and stains
Of generations that came before me
I came into this world already ruined
Absorbed all the shame and the hate
Through the cord that was supposed to
Feed me life and innocence
A gestational diet of unworthiness
Born already knowing the curses
As if they had been mine alone
Raised by two people broken by life
Both stained in early years
Stained by bruises from mother's hands
Stained by filth from brothers and
I ingested every self-judgment
Either of them carried
Feasted on the knowledge
No child should ever know
Born with a broken heart
Innocence was never mine
Spent childhood trying to
Save the people who made me
From themselves
From their hell
Grew up to be attracted
To the pains unspoken
Show them love, and hope
In vain, that they will give it back

But when a person doesn't love themselves
They are not capable of loving others
My heart breaks again and again
Trying to show love to those
Who cannot accept it
Like I am the sin eater absolving the living dead
Freeing their souls through a meal of pain
A meal I never wanted to eat
And an absolution I am not able to give
Desperately trying to show they are worthy
Regardless of what they've endured
All the while remembering
My gestational diet of unworthiness
For I am the baby of the family
Of the baby of the family
Carrying the scars and stains
Of generations that came
Before me
And I'm here to tell my familial ghosts

This shit stops HERE!

The truth is
everyone is going to hurt
you. You just got to find
the ones worth
        suffering for.

Bob Marley

Act 2
Relationships

Ultimately, our family teaches us about all other relationships in our lives. Friends, lovers, spouses, every relationship is approached with what we learned within the family.

Each subsequent relationship teaches us something more which we take into the next relationship. I've had good relationships and some that are not so good. In each case, I am responsible for my choices and live with my consequences – good or not.

I am eternally grateful for everything.

Toni B.

A Rose

(1984 – high school sophomore)

A rose is a beautiful friendship
A rose is a long-lasting love
A rose is an admiration
A feeling no others can touch

A rose is a most precious arrangement
It's cherished forever it seems
It stands for love and beauty
A rose makes all eyes gleam

But there comes a time, a season
When the feeling ends for no reason
The friendship is shattered
The love, then, it's tattered
And the end of your life seems so near
The reason for this is never quite clear
But it happens to everyone at least one
        Time in their life
The one beauteous rose leaves you
        Filled with strife

Yes, the rose is a most painful flower
There's a time it will hurt you but
        You don't know the hour
It pricks at your heart 'til you start
        To bleed
And you feel that death is how you'll be freed
Yes, the rose is a most painful flower.

Floating

When I was about seven years old
My father took me out to the pool
He had put up in our back yard
Just a small 4-foot-deep pool
For his family to enjoy
He stood, waist deep in the water
He picked me up in both arms
And laid me across the water
He told me to relax
I obliged because I knew my daddy had me
"I'm going to teach you how to float."
My daddy told me
"Swimming is good but floating will save your life."
I was only seven and I did not fully understand
But I trusted my daddy and his strong hands
"If you are ever in a boat that sinks,"
My daddy explained
"And you are far from land, if you try to swim
You will get too tired, and you could drown.
But if you float, you will be able to wait for help.
Floating will save your life."
I listened and I laid there on top of the water
Slowly, my daddy took his arms away
There I was, floating
'Twas a valuable lesson my daddy taught me
And yet, I have been swimming fiercely
Through life for so many years
With the tide, against the tide
Pulled by the undertow
Spit out on the sand
Freestyle, breaststroke, back stroke, side stroke
Doggy paddle, sometimes merely treading water
I've been exhausted from swimming

27

Toni B.

But I cannot swim with you
No matter what stroke I try, I drown a little
No, I cannot swim with you
Though your waters run deep
They cannot be stirred by the motion of swim
The only way to be with you
Is to relax, float, and ride the tide
Swimming is good but floating will save your life

Paper Plate

Classic Chinette
It's how the good times are plated.
Designed to handle the largest helpings
And sauciest sides
That's the line of paper plate
I am
Classic, white, strong
I am the paper plate for your dinner
Convenient and supportive
You hold me in your hands
And pile everything onto me
I bear the weight of your fodder
As you enjoy every bite
Licking your lips and fingers
Scraping every last morsel from my surface
The unsung hero of your party
I support the meal
But am not good enough to
Be proper China
Appreciated, but not kept
I'm unintrusive, unassuming
I don't force my way onto your table
You choose me over heirloom plates
Not willing to wash and return to
I am always clean and ready
Whether you want a quick snack
Or complete meal
Ah, yes, Chinette
Made with at least 80% recycled material
Proudly made in the U.S.A.
No bends or leaks, so load it up!

Toni B.

Dessert, lunch, dinner, compartment
Tray, bowl, napkin
Whichever size, shape, or use you require
Classic Chinette is what you reach for
Because you want something solid
A plate you can count on
Strong enough to handle whatever you need
While you need it
But ultimately cast aside without thought
For we are living in a disposable world
And I am a disposable girl...
[sung to the tune of Material Girl by Madonna]

Justice

He finally made me angry enough
To take a swing at him
He ducked, I missed
He threw me down the hallway
Then picked me up by the throat
Held me against the wall
With clenched fist drawn
I closed my eyes and held my breath
Felt my broken necklace fall
I heard his mother call
From the end of the hall
She didn't say stop
No, she said, "I think
We're looking at our
Next daughter-in-law"
My body went limp
My heart sank
I already knew if I tried to leave
He would kill my entire family
So, I stayed far too long
Plotting a way to
Escape the sleepless nights
The horrible fights
The guns shot inside the house
So many times, I didn't even flinch anymore
Plan the wedding
Plot my escape
I'll either leave or die trying
In complete exhaustion
I called my brother to pick me up from work

Toni B.

My car had been wrecked, again
Though I begged and cried for him to take me back
My brother wouldn't leave me there
My fear ran fast
I knew he would kill us all
Seen too much violence to not believe
The threats I was constantly told
Then a year after my escape
I finally got the call
He died last night
Single gunshot
Serves you right
You son of a bitch
Finally, justice

Life and Love for Free

You didn't realize it
But permission is what you gave
When you took that first punch
You thought you were being brave
You stood back up and faced him
Then came his deeper rage
He was the greatest charmer
Fell in with pure intent
Though he was clearly troubled
You knew what he really meant
He just needed you
To love him enough to see
The greatness within him
But that might never be
Then came the silver tongue
That taught you something new
No one had ever spoken
With such an interesting view
So, you took time to understand
And forgave so many things
Because if you just hang in there
He'll see true beauty rings
Little by little his lies became your truth
When you hear the same things over
You begin to believe them too
Then everything you thought you knew
Seemed silly and mundane
A glimmer of the man you met
Remains amidst the pain
If you can just keep getting up

He will eventually see
He has the greatest treasure
In the simple form of me
You know you can take it
Even though you shouldn't, dear
But if you stand and hold on
You'll save someone else from fear
After a time, you can see how
It has all been your own fault
He told you what you did wrong
And punished with assault
And after all this time
You must just try to do better
And save yourself from punishment
Or he may never unfetter
The vicious circle never ends
For each correction made
Brings up a new infraction
Left hook, she's down again
You look around and reach for help
But the only person there
Is the one that put you on the ground
So, you think no one else cares
That's what he keeps on telling you
And you guess it must be right
Though he won't let you walk outside
Because you might see the light
Somewhere along this crazy road
You forgot your reality
And he saw the greatest opportunity
To drag you to your knees
While you are down there crying

Think back to who you were
She is still within you
And **she** can break this curse
Because the truth is you didn't ask for this
You just wanted to love and be loved
But he cannot see you through
The anger-knife that draws your blood
And you meekly gave permission
With the first punch that you took
It may not have even been from him
Until you can wipe the tears and truly look
Your lovely truth will remain hidden
It is still there inside your heart
Fan the flame of your true self
And make a brand-new start
Lord knows it isn't easy
Nothing worth it ever is
The fear has held you captive
It's harder now, with kids
Is this the life you want for them?
They love you despite it all
Don't let his lies become their truth
Answer the freedom call
If you cannot see your worth
Please see the worth in them
Life doesn't have to work this way
I know you make excuses
I've made the same ones before
Kind hearts see good in ruthless
The path back to the truth in you
Is a long and winding road
But I promise you can walk it now

Lay down this treacherous load
I know you have been carrying it
And you think it is your lot
That's only if you accept it so
I can see that it is not
I reach out to you with compassion
I have no space to judge
I've walked that road you're traveling
I'm here to give a nudge
Remember you are worthy
Of life and love for free
If you can't see it yet
Just turn and look at me
I'll do my best to show you
What you truly are
Speak truth to you along the way
Until you're shining like a star
You've got this girl, I know it
It is your greatest mission
To tell the world it can be done
And they no longer have permission
To treat you as someone less than
Because you are so much more
It all begins with you, my dear
Believe and you will soar
Speak your own truth in the mirror
Not the lies he fed you
Speak courage 'til it comes clearer
Can you see her peeking through?
She's beautiful and capable
A light in this dark place

Take one step then another
You can run and win this race
And when you stumble here or there
Just look over at me
I'll do my best to remind you
You are worth life and love for free

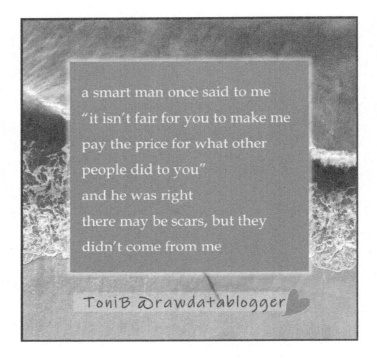

a smart man once said to me
"it isn't fair for you to make me
pay the price for what other
people did to you"
and he was right
there may be scars, but they
didn't come from me

ToniB @rawdatablogger

… I married that smart man

False Positive

False Positive
a test result which incorrectly indicates that
a particular condition or attribute is present
Like your love

To calculate the rate of false positives.
You take the number of false positive results (c)
And divide it by the total number of absences (c+d)
So, the rate of false positives = c / (c+d)

In other words, if I take the number of times
I have asked the universe if you love me (x)
And the universe said yes every time
But then divide that by the total number of
Damn this gets so confusing

So how can I ever know the answer
To the equation of love
Because how can you even begin to
Calculate infinity

And what number can you give
To measure the love I have for you?
For the only limiting equation
For the entire calculation
Is the amount of love I have for myself

Toni B.

False positive
a test result which incorrectly indicates that
a particular condition or attribute is present
Like my love

Price of Admission

The spotlights are shining
Toward the sky in electric circles
Red velvet ropes in mazes
Hopeful, beautiful people await
To see if they are beautiful enough
To gain access to this exclusive event
The air is palpable
Eager anticipation and hopefulness
Fill the air so thickly it is hard to breathe

At least a hundred have arrived ahead of me
At least a hundred more lined up behind
The line moves so slowly
As each is meticulously reviewed
Looked up and down, turn around
Quickly dismissed, not what you're looking for
Some gain small talk but are still turned away
Others are awarded conversation
Tasted for a moment and found not to your liking
But the ones with just the right look
The ones with both brains and beauty
They are allowed in for the show
How long it lasts, no one ever knows

When I finally arrive at the
Long awaited entrance
I stand tall and smile pretty
Take my spin and await the verdict
Small talk leads to conversation
A taste leads to a ticket to the show

Toni B.

The curtain rises, the house lights dim
Music stirs emotions long ago retired
And you pick me out of the crowd
Offer your hand and ask me to dance

I accept and we dance
First the tango – the dance of lovers
The tango was followed by a waltz
We kept dancing through every dance
We had ever known
As the orchestra played and the
House lights kept time

And I forgot completely about
The hundreds more waiting in line
Behind me, I just enjoyed the show
Occasionally wondering if it was real
Then questioning if the dance was
Worth the price of admission

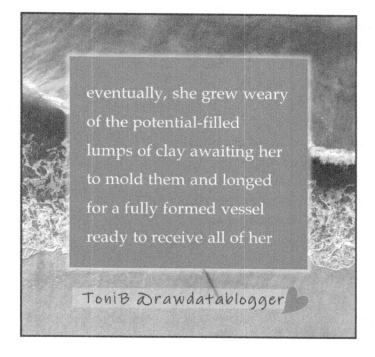

eventually, she grew weary
of the potential-filled
lumps of clay awaiting her
to mold them and longed
for a fully formed vessel
ready to receive all of her

ToniB @rawdatablogger

A Piece of Me

I have amazing love
For you
I see so many amazing
Things when I look at you
I wish you every happiness
With each breath you take away
I get lost in the deep conversations
When we talk about anything real
A piece of me dies with strained small talk

I have amazing love
For you
Your voice stirs pieces of my soul
I had kept in hiding for years
The way you have guided the tour of a world
That is new to me is so intoxicating
I drink it in, and everything spins
A piece of me dies each time I take a sip

I have amazing love
For you
My hopeful heart peeks cautiously
When you call and ask me out
I am lulled into peaceful sleep
By the rhythm of your soft snores
The morning view of you
Shines golden in the sunrise
A piece of me dies each time I leave your bed

I have amazing love
For you
And while I do not cling to regret
I am aware how many pieces of me
Have died in your hands
I am aware that when we met
I needed you to love me
I am aware that now I have amazing love
For me
And I cannot settle for
A piece of you

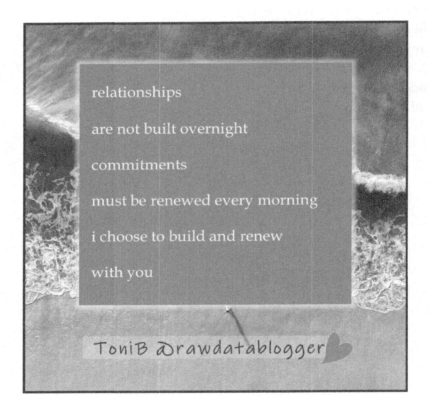

relationships

are not built overnight

commitments

must be renewed every morning

i choose to build and renew

with you

ToniB @rawdatablogger

Nantucket

"Before you die", I told my husband,
"You must take me to Nantucket
for two weeks in the fall."
It's the one place I'd always dreamt of
How that New England island called
But every three-day weekend
Holiday and vacation
Found us packing up the car
And driving west, not east
We'd drive for three hours plus
To arrive at the same place
Northwest Indiana, his hometown
With his parents we would stay
They were always glad to see us
And sad to see us leave
Whether after three days or two weeks
The departure was the same
I would drive and he would cry
Thinking he may not see them again
Year one, year two, and so on
For the eighteen years of us
We made that same westward journey
I'd ask again in hope that once
We could be eastward bound
I knew we would enjoy it
If the time could just be found
But time is ever fleeting and doesn't like to wait
So back to Indiana for another family scape
Memorial Day weekend
Two thousand and eight

Toni B.

We made that trip again
But it wasn't quite the same
He'd been taking treatments
And they were taking a toll
I gladly drove us there and back
To spend as much time as we could
He didn't cry when we left that time
But my heart was breaking for him
The next time we would all be together
They would drive eastward
I'd take them one by one
To the room where he now lay
I can hear the sounds to this very day
Ventilator, monitors, and empty IV bags
Then finally the time had come
I laid down by his side
I held him while I let him go
The hardest decision of my life
But I made sure his family was there
So he could go in peace with love
Surrounding everything
We never made it to Nantucket
And I'm alright with that
I didn't realize when I asked
How little time we had
But the island was still calling me
Though it never called to him
And so, I took myself a trip
A year after he passed
For fifteen nights I frolicked there
And learned to breathe again

My Entire Life

My entire life was ending
I went to him and held his hand
I cried from the depths of hell
A cry from every fiber of us
I don't know what it sounded like
Nothing else existed
Just him and I and that never ending cry
Time ceased—frozen—was it minutes or hours
I have no idea
I only know that I was completely
Submerged in the drowning of tears
The waters were pounding in my ears
And I was going under
The current was so strong
And I was immersed
I could not see the surface
My feet could not feel the bottom
My breath was gone
Then from out of nowhere
Two hands reached out of the depths
And held my shoulders
With a strength and softness that saved me
My lifeguard snatched me from the undertow
I didn't know anyone was there
I couldn't lift my head to see
But I could feel her energy
For just as I reached the blackest depth
Two hands held fast my registry

Toni B.

My mother's hands holding me
And my entire life
I will never know
What that did to her...

When it seems that
our sorrow is too great to
be borne, let us think of the
great family of the heavy-hearted
into which our grief has given us
entrance, and inevitably we will
feel about us their arms,
their sympathy, their
understanding.

Helen Keller

Act 3
Grief

The strongest relationship in my life was with my husband, Don. He was my best friend, my champion, my voice of reason, and the biggest pain in my ass. After being married for eleven years, one day he said to me, "Hun, you know there's only one thing I really don't like about you." I thought that was pretty good, one thing after eleven years. When I asked him what that one thing was, he told me it was my temper. I smiled and said, "That's pretty easy then, don't piss me off." And we laughed, because he knew he could do that quicker and more efficiently than anyone else on the planet.

The years since he passed have been challenging and they haven't always been graceful. But it's a process.

I am eternally grateful for everything.

Toni B.

A Death in the Family (October 1982 – age 13)

There's an empty feeling now
The place seems non-existent, how?

I'd rather not sit in his favorite chair
I'd rather just remember him there

Now it's as if he's watching over my shoulder
And since he's not here, it feels so much colder

I always longed to hear his praise
But now, for him, my voice will raise

To me he still is very alive
To meet him again, my soul will strive

But between now and then
The thoughts will mend
The tears of his loss
And the roads to be crossed

I've seen him and others dear to me
Disappear as a death in the family

If You Need Anything

So many people
Came up to say
"If you need anything
Just let me know"
They all mean well
I realize this
But my grace has run thin
I smile and say thank you
Because if I said more
It would not be gracious

But what I would have
Liked to say is,
"I need to go home
To my husband
And make dinner
Like I have for 18 years
I need to be his wife
I need to continue our life
Can you help me with that?
I didn't think so."

I stand here
Beside this casket
And I greet you
I say thank you for coming
I can't count the times
"I've heard "I'm so sorry for your loss."

Toni B.

My loss? Is that what this is?
My loss?
How simplistic to think that

But you don't understand
How could you?
You've never been where I stand
And so, I comfort you
And stand composed
The new widow
Epitome of grace
Thank you so much for coming

Here it comes again
"If you need anything
Blah, blah, blah"
I don't even know what day it is
And you expect me to know what I need?
I can't feel anything except
This gaping wound
Where I have been sawn from the
Top of my head
Vertically down through my body
With a rusty saw blade
And my right side has been
Gutted, then dressed and pressed
And tucked neatly in a box
That I stand beside
And greet you all
With half of me missing

If you need anything
Yes, thank you, I have no fucking idea
But I hope by saying it **you** somehow feel better
Trust me, I won't call
I can't call
I wouldn't know what to say if I did
And I don't have the strength to
Pick up the phone anyway
Thank you for coming

"If you need someone to talk to,
I've been through divorce,
So, I understand loss."
Bitch, please, back it up
Did I mention I have this huge
Gaping wound that you just
Threw a pound of salt into?
You don't have a clue
There is no comparison between the two
But you mean well
Thank you for coming
I need to go speak to someone over there

If you need anything
Right, I can tell you a couple of things
I don't need
I don't need pity
And I don't need you to not speak about him
And I don't need $100 in drug store
Coupons saying, we want you back
If $100 is all it takes, I'll pay that

Toni B.

I don't need you to bring food
I'm not eating much these days
I'll just sit here with my
Six friends and drink myself to sleep
Leave a message
I can't pick up the phone right now

Message retrieved
Three days later
If you need anything
Got it. Thank you for calling
Message deleted

Back to work
Not actually working, but there
"Hi, I was wondering how I could pray for you"
I'm instantly pissed,
Not because of the question
But because of who asked it
And the way it was asked
Dripping with pity and
You know we don't have that relationship
You mean well, I suppose
But damn, really?
Praying doesn't require
You to ask me how
Nor you to show up with your
Self-righteous ass to feel good about
Your sociopathic care
But since you asked
And my grace has completely
Gone by the wayside

Sure, I'll tell you
Why don't you pray that
People would stop trying to
Keep me in a place I don't want to be
How about you pray that people
Would let me move on
And live my life
How about you pray on that?

Ok, but if you need anything...
Yeah, got it
Thank you for coming
I'm sorry for being so angry
I'm sure you are all hurting as well
I know that it isn't easy to come
To these things and all you want to do
Is comfort my pain, ease your pain
It must seem like there isn't anything
Anyone can say or do that is alright
I'm sorry for that
But I have never been here before either
And my grace has left me
I do so appreciate everything
Even though it cannot change anything
I love the friend who waited in line
Just to hug me so tight and say "love you"
Because he knew there are no words
For these times, only presence in the moment
And forgiveness for all the awkward
Exchanges of well wishes
I love the neighbor who didn't ask
But came over and mowed my lawn

Toni B.

It never occurred to me to do it
I love the friends who appeared from
Spaces I would have never expected
And the graceful exit of the friends
It now hurts too much to see
I love the stories of this man that I never heard before
Thank you for knowing him and seeing him
I hate the secrets I keep and the worry I carry
But I am truly grateful
For everything
For even my anger can be a purification of sorts
But I've held onto this anger for far too long
Fearing that if I am no longer his wife
Who am I now?
Thank you for coming.
If you need anything, just let me know.

The Anger

Where do you put
Your anger
When there is no one to be angry with
There was no drunk driver
No malicious intent
There was no shooter
No breaking and entering
Except for the cancer
That broke into your mind
And entered our lives
It snuck in without invitation
Claimed squatter's rights in your brain
Made itself at home
Grew comfortable in our space
Then became bold enough to
Announce its presence
Like the flick of a light switch
Not at stage one, or two
No, this is stage four
Glioblastoma multiforme
Grade four astrocytoma
It makes you sound ornate
No time to be angry now
Must find a way to hope
Focus on healing
Focus on care
Focus on the blessings
They are truly everywhere
If no treatment means six months
Then treatment must mean more

Toni B.

But with everything we did to hope
It only gave you four
But where do I put my anger
When there is no one to be angry with
Because the cancer doesn't care
And no one deserves to bear
The brunt of my fury
So, I swallowed it
Denied it because it wasn't fair
For a time, I didn't even realize
My anger was still there
I have to get it out of me
The only way I know
I cast to an empty page
Bleed it out in ink and rage
For where else can you put
The anger when there's
No one to be angry with?

I Wear Dresses

I typically wear dresses
It's a matter of comfort
It's a matter of ease
Actually, it was a necessity
It's a thing I started to do
After my husband died
When I couldn't pick out
A complete outfit
It was too taxing
A dress is always going
To match itself
You don't have to tuck it in
Just put it on and go
I typically wear dresses
Because I can no longer
Match my clothes
For almost twenty years
He bought every outfit I owned
He told me when something didn't flatter
He told me when I looked good
He once flew from New Jersey
With a big box from Macy's
As his carry-on luggage
Because it was my birthday
And he had bought me an outfit
I typically wear dresses
After thirteen years
They are all I know how to wear

Nobody Said it was Easy

The path of self-discovery is not for the faint of heart. It isn't for people who can't look at themselves honestly, who cannot strip away the masks and filters to see what is absolutely true about themselves. It isn't always pretty, and it is not easy, but it is absolutely beautiful...absolutely amazing. With each realization comes understanding...growth.

While I love to have deep conversations with people, the person I speak with most frequently is myself. Since the onset of this COVID-19 pandemic, I have been able to look inward at great lengths. I have been able to step back from the day-to-day and truly question my choices and habits and patterns more deeply. The self-discovery of 2020 has been pivotal and, yet, difficult. There are days when I succumb to the struggle – days when I cry – days I am a raw human. For a moment, I take off my crown, and sit with the questions and feel even more deeply than normal.

Yesterday was one of those days. I was troubled in my soul. The struggle sat me down and fell from my eyes. I sat on a bench on the Virginia Beach Boardwalk at 23rd Street and was completely alone, closed off, introspective. I reached out to a friend and was asked if I needed anything. I said I didn't know. Then, I said, "I guess I do need something...a friend." A few minutes later, the first friend I made here arrived, sat down next to me, put his arm around me and asked me why I had tears. At first, I didn't really know how to articulate that.

My friend sat beside me, music playing in the background, and patiently waited for me to be able to find my words. It's a pretty big realization day when I can't find my words. Little by little, I started to share random things that had been rattling around in my mind. Things like why I have body image issues, how I've never been in my current position before, how I always give so much and never receive, how I work so hard at everything. Just small things that weren't really what I was on my way to discovering at all...just thoughts that were present. And yet, we sat there for a few hours, sometimes in silence as I stared at the ocean enveloped in my process of discovery.

After the fog rolled in and out, then in again, my friend asked me if I was ready to walk. So, we started south down the boardwalk, music in tow. Another friend was coming to the boardwalk as well but had not arrived. As we walked by 20th Street, I paused to take a picture of the weather for our friend. We continued walking and turned onto 11th Street. My friend decided we needed a margarita and some fajitas, he's a good friend. He continued to allow me to dance between smiles and tears. As our food arrived, our friend also arrived at the beach, then walked to meet us at the South Side Cantina. The three of us enjoyed simple conversation and the presence of one another. It was sweet and I felt quietly comforted sitting between these two people yet was still visibly working toward my discovery. They didn't pry, they just stayed present.

We gathered our things and returned to the boardwalk, claiming a bench at 20th Street. The music played, there was small conversation, and I could feel both of these men just sitting alongside to make sure I was alright. They still did not pry, but only stayed present...such a gift! I chose a few songs to be played and closed my eyes to sing along. The last song I chose was "She Don't Want Nobody Near" by Counting Crows. As the song completed, I started to realize something I have known for 12 years in a new way. It may sound simple, but it isn't. It hit me so hard that I had to walk away from my friends and pace and allow the idea to consume me in a new way. I returned to the bench only to get back up and pace some more. They were both concerned. My first friend caught up with me and asked if I was alright. My other friend looked on and stayed present, not wanting to push. Again, I couldn't find my words. And so, they both waited quietly.

A few minutes later, I just had to leave. My first friend asked if I was ready to go, yes. My second friend asked me if I was alright, yes. My first friend gathered his bike with the music and, as usual, walked alongside me to my car. My second friend (literally the order I met them) said he was going to stay there for a little longer and would check on me later. Neither of them had any idea what I had going on in my head.

Again, I know that it sounds simple, but it isn't. I am a widow. I became a widow at the age of 39. My husband died in my arms because I promised him he'd never be alone. I have spent years choosing to live, working to become, and trying not to be defined by this label. I never wanted to be a widow, least of all before the age of 40, but that's what I am. The final stage of grief, they say, is acceptance. Yesterday, I swallowed the idea whole. Yesterday, I came to accept. Yesterday, I cried, again. Yesterday, two friends who know nothing about what it means to be a widow, quietly and eloquently came alongside, and helped me discover something without even knowing what they did.

I am eternally grateful in ways immeasurable for yesterday. But today is a new day...let's do this. Peace...

What a Difference a Day Makes

Today is September 24, 2020. Today is Thursday. Today is overcast. Today is just a day. Except that it isn't. Twenty-six years ago, today was a Saturday. On that day, I got up early to have my hair done. My veil was positioned just perfectly into my hair – satin roses and a fingertip veil. I put on my mother's wedding dress that day. I walked down the aisle to my new life as Don's wife. What a difference a day makes.

It was 1994 and I was young and idealistic. I was happy to be starting this new life with this man who adored me. When I was 13 years old, at a family reunion, my uncle asked me when I thought I would get married. I didn't hesitate and told him I would get married when I was 25. That is exactly what I did. I was 25, Don was 28, and we were surrounded by friends and family. How could it get any better than this?

Our marriage lasted almost 14 years (though we were together for 18). The ups and down, the fighting and coming together, the laughter and the tears filled those years with a life that we built together. But then, in March 2008, we got the diagnosis. Glioblastoma multiforme grade 4 astrocytoma. Layman's terms, brain cancer. We did the treatments – seven weeks of chemo and radiation. I managed the medications – 22 different prescriptions. We saw the doctors from U of M in Ann Arbor to Toledo to local. We tried. We hoped. I called the ambulance the night of June 2. I stayed by his side. Then I laid down beside him, with his family all around, on June 11 and let him go. What a difference a day makes.

Toni B.

Today is September 24, 2020. Today is a Thursday. Today is overcast. Today is just a day. Except that it isn't. Because today will always be my anniversary. Happy anniversary, Don. Thank you for everything. Peace be with you.

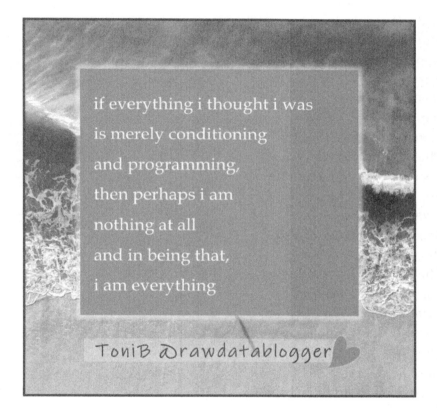

if everything i thought i was

is merely conditioning

and programming,

then perhaps i am

nothing at all

and in being that,

i am everything

ToniB @rawdatablogger

Toni B.

Plans for Dinner

I have plans for dinner
No, you may not join me
I must do this by myself
I choose a nice restaurant
I dress for a date
Order a cocktail
Maybe two
Appetizer, yes
Entrée
Dessert
Cappuccino
Savor every bite
This is a celebration
It's supposed to be a table
For two
I was supposed to
Receive a bouquet of roses
But they never came
I haven't gotten the deliveries
For the past 13 years
I was supposed to have
A small box wrapped by
The jeweler to open
Here at the table
This year would have been
Our 27th anniversary
But here I sit, alone
Thank you for a lovely dinner

I leave and drive home
Crawl into a single bed
Three pillows, two of which are you
Good night
See you next year
When I will make plans for dinner
With you, but without you

Smoke Screen

I smoke cigarettes
About a half a pack a day
It isn't very intelligent
Keeps getting in my way
I think about not smoking
That would be a better choice
These things are beginning to
Really affect my voice
So, I think about the why of it
Seems there must be a reason
Otherwise, I would not choose
To light these sticks of treason
I quit the habit for over 15 years
Couldn't stand to be around it
Then one day, you passed away
And I quickly returned to it
I remembered how you told me
You were so proud of me
You said the only time I smoked
Now is when you made me
And I took some consolation
In the idea that you knew
Then I read a book that seemed
To give me passage too
Because I never wanted
To have to wait too long for you
Anything that I could do
To put us back together
That you would understand
Made every cigarette another step in our plan

I toyed with quitting a couple of times
But it never really stuck
The times I feel the most alone
Are calmed by smoke and such
Then it became a way to
Get a break from work
Buried myself in my job
I never stopped to breathe
But if I smoked a cigarette
I had to go outside, to leave
When COVID hit, I didn't work
But I still made time to light them
Puffing every step back to you
Defying my inner sanctum
And as I grow within myself
Each cigarette, it mocks me
And stands between my truth
And the person I am choosing
For if I don't smoke anymore
What am I really saying?
That I no longer need you
Or is it dragons I am slaying
When I ask myself the question,
When no one is around
The answer I most loudly hear
Is you smoke to keep them out
The first thing potential suitors say
Is I don't like that you smoke
You said the same thing when we met
For me it's like a joke
Because you understand my whys
And they have no idea

But a part of me believes
I'm worth looking past the ruse
And maybe if the suitor can
See through my subterfuge
They'll be worth the love I give
When I truly do give in
But to do that for another man
Means I'm no longer with you
And so I light another one
And watch it burn in my own hand
Because it keeps me on the road
To be with you again
But maybe what I truly miss
Is that security
Someone to come home to
Giving perspective, clarity
And what I struggle with
Is being that for me

Heart Armor

My precious heart
Was broken – shattered
It wasn't anyone's fault
I didn't even realize it happened
I just knew you were gone
With that I lost myself
Because I became you
And you became me
That's how it was supposed to be
Then I laid down beside you
And you became whole again
Left your broken body behind
And hovered over me
But my heart couldn't handle
Being vulnerable
Like that again
I didn't even realize
I had put it on
Now I know
My heart armor is strong
I went through the motions
Pretended I could care
Unintentional disservice
To anyone who tried to
Love me
Even now I question
Can I take my armor off?
When is it safe to
Expose my heart

Toni B.

Perhaps never
Maybe just a piece can go
Test the water
Can I survive without
My heart armor?

Good-bye

I slowly reached around my neck
Unhooked the clasp that held you
Your thumbprint hanging on a chain
For all these years helped me get through

Whenever I needed you close
I reached up and caressed you
Hanging by my heartbeat
Holding onto a memory
Keeping in your company
A symbol of a life I lived
So many years ago
Built-in redemptive qualities
A role I played so well

I'm grateful for our story, dear
But I've got my own to tell
Thank you for watching over me
You've been patient for so long
It's time for me to set you free
I need to sing a brand-new song

The melody will come to me
With each new step I take
The harmonies will blend in time
With each new friend I make
I wish you peace in your journey
As I make peace with mine
Though it's hard to let you go

Toni B.

I know now is the time
So grateful for everything
I know love never dies
But life is for the living
Peace out, my love, good-bye

Where you grew up
becomes a big part of who
you are for the rest of your life
You can't run away from that.
Well, sometimes the running away
from it is what makes you
who you are.

Helen Mirren

Act 4
Run Away Home

It is said that the average person moves eleven times in their life. At the point of this writing, I am on address number 17 and contemplating my next move. No matter what address I am connected with, home will always be this flesh and blood temple where my spirit resides.

Through writing, I have tried to get out all the difficult bits and leave them on the paper. I know I cannot carry all of that around with me. But maybe someone out there will be helped by reading them and feel like they are not alone in their struggle.

Wherever you go, there you are. So, it's helpful to realize that in life you either win or you learn. You are on your way, and you are perfectly on time.

Be easy on yourself and keep putting one foot in front of the other.

Eternally grateful...always.

Toni B.

The Puzzle (undated poem circa 1986)

It twists, it turns
　　My heart it yearns
　　　　To find a clue
　　　　　　I wish I knew
　　　　　　　　The answers to life
　　　　　　　　　　And all of its strife
　　　　　　　　　　　　It's like a battle
　　　　　　　　　　　　　　An unceasing rattle
　　　　　　　　　　　　To which my mind
　　　　　　　　　　Soon hopes to find
　　　　　　　　A light, and end
　　　　　　To finish the bends
　　　　In science and health
　　Yes, to life itself
If there's a will, if a way,
　　An open shore on a bright bay
　　　　The pieces could fit
　　　　　　Unite just a bit
　　　　　　　　There might be a path
　　　　　　　　　　Among all this wrath
　　　　　　　　　　　　Of politics and such
　　　　　　　　　　　　　　Not too little nor too much
　　　　　　　　　　　　Just a little hint
　　　　　　　　　　So the road's not so bent
　　　　　　　　Maybe tonight
　　　　　　Yes, I just might
　　　　Find the answer to the p
　　　　　　　　　　　uz
　　　　　　　　　　　　　zle...

There Once Was a Girl

There once was a girl who didn't know her own strength, so she spent years asking other people to tell her. Tell me a story, she'd say, about the girl who didn't know her own strength. But the story would not be shared with her. She longed to hear it, yet she wasn't listening. So even if someone tried to tell it, it would not be accurate and would not be heard.

In search of the story, the girl would reach out and connect and try to see her reflection in the eyes of others. Every connection is a reflection of yourself in some way, she would say. You get what you give, so seeing yourself reflected back to you is of immense value. But the reality is that reflection is distorted through an alternate lens.

There once was a girl who didn't know her own strength. She spent years trying to devour information to increase her knowledge in an attempt to make sense of all things. The more you know, the more you grow, after all. But this, too, makes no sense. Because said information comes from another source with its own agenda. While it may be interesting, it may only be conjecture.

There once was a girl who didn't know her own strength, but she constructed a home out of the pain of others. If only she could help someone else, she too could be helped. She felt immense satisfaction in bringing hope and sunshine to people who were hurting. She would sacrifice the entirety of herself to help someone else. A servant heart, indeed, but at what cost?

There once was a girl who didn't know her own strength. She could not see her own beauty. She could not see that a martyr's life was truly no life at all. She got so heavily mired in the teachings, and the learnings, and the logic of everything that she forgot to listen to the music. For the music was free and easy and flowing and how could that be right?

There once was a girl who didn't know her own strength. She could see so clearly for everyone but herself. But really, she was talking to herself the entire time. It's the listening that was difficult. When she told someone to follow their heart – really, she was telling herself. When she told someone to not change their course for another – she was really telling herself. And when she asked someone what was stopping them from doing something – she was really asking herself.

There once was a girl who didn't know her own strength until she became quiet and realized that the song in her heart was her destiny. When she finally listened to her song, she heard the words – just go. When she contemplated an unknown journey without limitations, she knew that the cocoon she had woven for herself had to be discarded. It was time to become her beautiful butterfly self and go.

There once was a girl who didn't know her own strength. But she knew, however difficult, she must fly on her own. She knew she had to be near the sea, and she had to listen to her own song. With gratitude in her heart and unconditional love spilling as tears from her eyes, her time had come and so she will go.

What Happened?

She began the journey of a thousand miles to be by the ocean.
Setting out from Gary, Indiana and landing in Virginia Beach,
VA. She looked deeply inside herself and realized that putting her
life on hold for a narrative that had to be forced through an
alternate story line was making her become stagnant and
frustrated. And so, she loaded her Ford Escape with only the
items she could lift by herself, and that fit in the car, and drove to
the ocean. It was there she found the courage to share her soul
with the world.

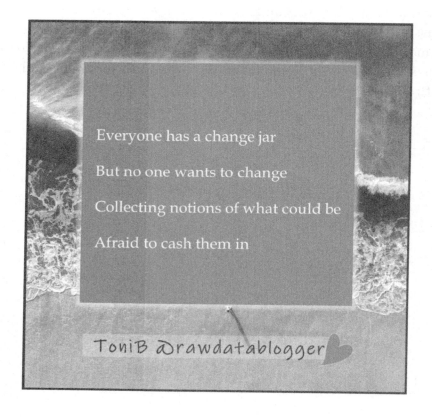

Everyone has a change jar

But no one wants to change

Collecting notions of what could be

Afraid to cash them in

ToniB @rawdatablogger

I Met Someone

I looked to the west
And looked to the east
I even looked up and then down
But nothing was right

I listened to pleas
And listened to lies
I even stopped listening
Not wanting to hear

I hoped to feel pretty
Hoped to feel care
Hoped against hope
Fell into despair

And then out of nowhere
It finally happened
I met someone
While I wasn't looking

It happened like a slow birth
And happened in a glance
I caught a look that
Stopped me in my track

It happened in the mirror
As I turned and looked
I met the one I searched for
I met the love in me

I Met Someone II

I met someone
And she is ME
Funny I've been here all along
But never thought myself enough
To sing a complete song

I met someone
And she is ME
The mirror has finally spoken true
What I used to see in there
Had holes through and through

I met someone
And she is ME
The holes shine my light
From every single source of pain
I've grown to my delight

I met someone
And she is ME
Not the youth of pain and angst
But the beauty of experience
And truth that lights my way

I met someone
And She is ME
Strong and fragile all at once
Feeling love and gratitude
Accepting all that is and was

I met someone
And SHE IS ME
Small in frame but large in heart
Beautifully flawed and talented
With wings to fly and courage to part
I met someone
And SHE IS ME

Toni B.

Trust the Journey

Silly girl
Don't you know
It was all perfect
Just the way it should go

The heartaches
The silence
Self-imposed guilt
Walls of defense

All of the choices
Were yours to make
It's the consequences
That were hard to take

But what of the lessons
Along the way?
All coming together
Perfect stage play

Each act, each scene
Must take its own sweet time
Unfold as great stories do
You cannot rush nor force the rhyme

Take your mark at center stage
Stand tall and breathe deeply
Relax your body and your mind
Open your heart completely

For out of love life does flow
The beauty will surround you
Stop trying to plan everything
The universe will surprise you

Stand up, show up, do your part
Be true to your soul inside
All things exist to serve you well
They're just waiting for you to decide

Look back and see how every scene
Has brought you safely here
And trust that still small voice
To guide you as you fly, dear

You silly girl
Don't you know
It's all been perfect
Just how it should go

Me

(Rhythm and Poetry 2019)

I am all me
Unapologetically
Not hypothetically
It's just the real me

I'm not skinny
Only five foot three
But my feet touch the ground
They always carry me

I got 'em firmly planted
With my head in the sky
My foundation is solid
But I'm always gonna fly

I am all me
Unapologetically
Not hypothetically
It's just the real me

This world can't hold me
I've got bigger game
You can't keep up with this
But you'll remember my name

Love me, hate me
Please, it's all the same
Such a fine line, man
My strut tells you I'm not tame

People try to cage me
I'll have none of that
Won't let you cover my flame
Under no team hat

Dress me how you want to
But just remember this
My fire burns too brightly
Not down for any bullshit

I am all me
Unapologetically
Not hypothetically
I'm just the real me

Thank You

To every single soul
Who has joined me on this path
Whether you came and went
Or came and stayed
I thank you

I thank you for the love
And equally for the pain
For the conversation,
Perspective, and even the lies

When I look at all you taught me
The only thing I can be is
Grateful, truly I thank you

If your intent was pure
Or if you intentionally hurt
Everything was worth it
Because I am more
Thanks to you

I am stronger and wiser
than I was before you
But more than that
I am more grateful,
More humble, and more LOVE

To every single soul
Who touched my soul
THANK YOU

Run Away Home

Wherever you go
There you are
Standing flat foot
On the ground
Reaching for a star
Changing scenery
Changing plans
Always searching
Shifting sands
Peeling off labels
Attached along the way
Preacher's daughter
Prayer group leader
Wife
Widow
Who am I really?
Putting on the lifestyle
To see if this one fits
Too small
Too big
Too short
Too long
Changing
        Changing
                Changing
Can't find the right song
Pack it up
Move along
New address
New costume

Toni B.

Life really is a stage
I am the star
Of this production
But I don't have a script
Been looking for the director
He must have jumped this ship
The spotlight shines upon me
Can't see the audience
I stand here waiting for my line
Instead, I hear a whisper
Girl, you're right on time
Settle in and listen
The lines will come to you
You're not just the star
But the director too
The stage is here for you
The lighting is perfect
You'll have the best success
When you learn to just relax
The character you're playing
Is the one and only you
And no one can direct your show
They wouldn't know how to
But you will find your position
The script will become clear
When you understand that home
Is looking in your mirror

*Out beyond
ideas of wrongdoing
and rightdoing there is a field.
I'll meet you there. When the soul
lies down in that grass the world is
too full to talk about. Ideas, language,
even the phrase 'each other'
doesn't make any sense.*

Rumi

Conclusion

I know I don't have the answers. I have more questions than anything. Sometimes I wish I could have the secure knowledge I thought I had in my thirties. But I do not have that anymore.

I smile when I think of the person I thought I was back then. She was something! She knew right from wrong and up from down. She had so much clarity. She was so inane. I love her for who she was, but I would not go back. I have learned to love every person I have ever been and every lesson in the phases. Some days that love comes easier than others, for I am still on this journey.

This journey home is the same for everyone. Though our addresses may be different, we are all here to learn how to be love. We finally find home when we can love ourselves in this flesh and bone costume of this existence. When we become love within ourselves, we have only love to give to the world. Namaste...

~Toni B.

About the Author

Toni Lynn Britton was born and raised in Williams County Ohio, in the northwest corner of the state. She graduated from North Central High School in Pioneer, Ohio – the same school, same building, her mother graduated from 24 years prior.

Even as a child, she felt a call to be by the ocean on the East Coast – before she had ever seen an ocean or traveled anywhere. But life began and unfolded in the Midwest. Finally, at the age of 51, she packed up and drove east landing in Virginia Beach, VA. She didn't know anyone there, did not have a job, and did not have a place to live. But she was finally at the ocean and that is where she eventually found her voice, began her blog page, and found her church at The Venue on 35th in Norfolk. Eternally grateful for the journey thus far.

[original photo provided by @photobyunscripted follow on Instagram]

Toni B.

<u>Colophon</u>

Brought to you by Wider Perspectives Publishing, care of James Wilson, with the mission of advancing the poetry and creative community of Hampton Roads, Virginia.
This page used to have many cute and poetic expressions, but the sheer number of quality artists deserving mention has superseded the need to art. This has become some serious business; please check out how *They art...*

Se'Mon Rosser
Nick Marickovich
Grey Hues
Madeline Garcia
Chichi Iwuorie
Symay Rhodes
Tanya Cunningham-Jones
　　　　(Scientific Eve)
Terra Leigh
Raymond M. Simmons
Samantha Borders-Shoemaker
Taz Weysweete'
Jade Leonard
Darean Polk
Bobby K.
　　　　(The Poor Man's Poet)
J. Scott Wilson (Teech!)
Charles Wilson
Gloria Darlene Mann
Neil Spirtas
Jorge Mendez & JT Williams
Sarah Eileen Williams
Stephanie Diana (Noftz)
Shanya – Lady S.
Jason Brown (Drk Mtr)
Ken Sutton

Crickyt J. Expression
Lisa M. Kendrick
Cassandra IsFree
Nich (Nicholis Williams)
Samantha Geovjian Clarke
Natalie Morison-Uzzle
Gus Woodward II
Patsy Bickerstaff
Edith Blake
Jack Cassada
Dezz
Catherine TL Hodges
Kent Knowlton
Linda Spence-Howard
Tony Broadway
Zach Crowe
Mark Willoughby
Martina Champion
... and others to come soon.

the Hampton Roads
　　　　Artistic Collective
　　　　(757 Perspectives) &
The Poet's Domain
are all WPP literary journals in cooperation with Scientific Eve or Live Wire Press

Check for those artists on FaceBook, Instagram, the Virginia Poetry Online channel on YouTube, and other social media.

Hampton Roads Artistic Collective is an extension of WPP which strives to simultaneously support worthy causes in Hampton Roads and the local creative artists.